EMMANUEL JOSEPH

Unraveling the Inner Maze: A Guide to Self-Discovery

Copyright © 2025 by Emmanuel Joseph

All rights reserved. No part of this publication may be reproduced, stored or transmitted in any form or by any means, electronic, mechanical, photocopying, recording, scanning, or otherwise without written permission from the publisher. It is illegal to copy this book, post it to a website, or distribute it by any other means without permission.

First edition

This book was professionally typeset on Reedsy.
Find out more at reedsy.com

Contents

1	Chapter 1: The Journey Begins	1
2	Chapter 2: Understanding Your Past	3
3	Chapter 3: Embracing Your Present	5
4	Chapter 4: Uncovering Your True Self	7
5	Chapter 5: Overcoming Limiting Beliefs	9
6	Chapter 6: Embracing Change	11
7	Chapter 7: Building Resilience	13
8	Chapter 8: Cultivating Self-Compassion	15
9	Chapter 9: Setting Intentions and Goals	17
10	Chapter 10: Embracing Gratitude	19
11	Chapter 11: Finding Your Purpose	21
12	Chapter 12: Embracing the Journey	23

1

Chapter 1: The Journey Begins

Embarking on the path of self-discovery is akin to navigating a maze. This maze is filled with twists, turns, and dead ends, but it is also full of hidden treasures and moments of enlightenment. The journey begins with a single step - the decision to look inward and seek understanding. This first chapter will guide you through the initial stages of self-reflection, helping you to identify the aspects of your life that you wish to explore and understand.

As you take these first steps, it is important to approach the process with an open mind and a willingness to confront both the positive and negative aspects of yourself. This journey is not about perfection, but rather about gaining a deeper understanding of who you are and what drives you. By embracing this mindset, you will be better equipped to navigate the challenges that lie ahead.

One of the most crucial aspects of beginning this journey is setting aside time for self-reflection. This may involve journaling, meditation, or simply spending time alone in thought. Whatever method you choose, the goal is to create a space where you can explore your thoughts and feelings without judgment. This practice will help you to develop a greater sense of self-awareness and provide a foundation for the discoveries to come.

Finally, remember that the journey of self-discovery is a lifelong process. There is no finish line, and the insights you gain along the way will continue to evolve as you grow and change. Embrace the journey and be patient with yourself as you navigate the inner maze.

2

Chapter 2: Understanding Your Past

To truly understand yourself, it is essential to examine your past. Our experiences, both positive and negative, shape who we are and influence our thoughts, feelings, and behaviors. This chapter will guide you through the process of reflecting on your past and uncovering the patterns and themes that have shaped your life.

Begin by considering the key events and experiences that have had a significant impact on you. These may include childhood memories, relationships, successes, and failures. As you reflect on these experiences, try to identify the emotions and thoughts that accompanied them. Understanding how these events have influenced you can provide valuable insights into your current beliefs and behaviors.

Next, explore the patterns and themes that emerge from your reflections. Are there recurring experiences or emotions that have shaped your life? Identifying these patterns can help you to understand the underlying factors that drive your thoughts and actions. For example, if you notice a pattern of fear or insecurity, you can begin to explore the root causes of these feelings and work towards addressing them.

It is also important to consider the role of external influences in shaping your past. These may include family, friends, culture, and societal expectations. Understanding how these influences have impacted you can help you to separate your true self from the external pressures that may have shaped your beliefs and behaviors.

Finally, as you reflect on your past, remember to approach the process with compassion and understanding. Our past experiences, both positive and negative, have contributed to who we are today. Embrace your past as a valuable part of your journey and use the insights you gain to inform your path forward.

3

Chapter 3: Embracing Your Present

The present moment is where true self-discovery happens. By focusing on the here and now, you can gain a deeper understanding of your current thoughts, feelings, and behaviors. This chapter will guide you through the process of embracing the present moment and using it as a tool for self-discovery.

Begin by practicing mindfulness, which is the act of paying attention to the present moment without judgment. This can be achieved through various techniques, such as deep breathing, meditation, or simply paying attention to your surroundings. By practicing mindfulness, you can develop a greater awareness of your thoughts and feelings, allowing you to gain valuable insights into your inner world.

As you become more aware of your present thoughts and feelings, take the time to explore them without judgment. Ask yourself questions such as: What am I feeling right now? What thoughts are running through my mind? What is driving my current behavior? By examining your present experiences, you can begin to uncover the underlying factors that influence your actions and emotions.

In addition to mindfulness, it is important to engage in activities that bring you joy and fulfillment. These activities can help you to connect with your true self and provide a sense of purpose and meaning. Whether it is spending time with loved ones, pursuing a hobby, or engaging in self-care practices, make time for the activities that nourish your soul.

Finally, remember that embracing the present moment is an ongoing practice. It requires patience, self-compassion, and a willingness to confront your inner world. By continually practicing mindfulness and engaging in activities that bring you joy, you can develop a deeper understanding of yourself and continue to grow on your journey of self-discovery.

4

Chapter 4: Uncovering Your True Self

At the core of self-discovery is the quest to uncover your true self. This involves peeling back the layers of societal expectations, external influences, and self-imposed limitations to reveal the authentic you. This chapter will guide you through the process of uncovering your true self and embracing your unique identity.

Begin by examining the roles and identities you have adopted throughout your life. These may include roles such as student, employee, parent, or friend. While these roles are an important part of your life, they do not define who you are at your core. Take the time to explore how these roles have influenced your beliefs and behaviors, and consider whether they align with your true self.

Next, identify the values and beliefs that are most important to you. These are the guiding principles that shape your decisions and actions. By understanding your core values, you can begin to make choices that align with your true self and lead to a more fulfilling life. Take the time to reflect on what truly matters to you and how you can incorporate these values into your daily life.

In addition to examining your roles and values, it is important to explore your passions and interests. These are the activities and pursuits that bring you joy and fulfillment. By engaging in activities that align with your passions, you can connect with your true self and experience a greater sense of purpose and meaning.

Finally, remember that uncovering your true self is an ongoing process. As you grow and change, your understanding of your true self may evolve. Embrace this journey with an open mind and a willingness to continually explore and discover new aspects of yourself.

5

Chapter 5: Overcoming Limiting Beliefs

Limiting beliefs are the negative thoughts and assumptions that hold us back from reaching our full potential. These beliefs often stem from past experiences, societal expectations, and self-imposed limitations. This chapter will guide you through the process of identifying and overcoming these limiting beliefs, allowing you to move forward on your journey of self-discovery.

Begin by identifying the limiting beliefs that are holding you back. These may include thoughts such as "I'm not good enough," "I can't do this," or "I don't deserve success." Take the time to reflect on these beliefs and consider where they come from. Are they based on past experiences or external influences? Understanding the root of these beliefs can help you to challenge and overcome them.

Next, challenge your limiting beliefs by examining the evidence for and against them. Are these beliefs based on facts or assumptions? Are there examples of times when you have succeeded despite these beliefs? By challenging your limiting beliefs, you can begin to see them for what they are - false assumptions that no longer serve you.

In addition to challenging your limiting beliefs, it is important to replace them with positive and empowering beliefs. These are the thoughts and assumptions that support your growth and success. For example, replace "I'm not good enough" with "I am capable and deserving of success." By adopting positive beliefs, you can create a mindset that supports your journey of self-discovery.

Finally, remember that overcoming limiting beliefs is an ongoing process. It requires patience, persistence, and self-compassion. As you continue to challenge and replace your limiting beliefs, you will begin to see new possibilities and opportunities for growth and self-discovery.

6

Chapter 6: Embracing Change

Change is an inevitable part of life and an essential aspect of self-discovery. By embracing change, you can open yourself up to new experiences and opportunities for growth. This chapter will guide you through the process of embracing change and using it as a tool for self-discovery.

Begin by acknowledging the importance of change in your life. Change allows you to grow, adapt, and evolve, leading to new insights and perspectives. Embrace the idea that change is a natural and necessary part of your journey, and be open to the possibilities it brings.

Next, develop a mindset that is open to change. This involves cultivating a sense of curiosity and a willingness to explore new experiences. By approaching change with an open mind, you can develop a greater sense of resilience and adaptability. This mindset will help you to navigate the challenges and uncertainties that come with change.

In addition to developing an open mindset, it is important to take proactive steps to embrace change in your life. This may involve setting new goals, exploring new interests, or making changes to your daily routine. By actively seeking out new experiences, you can continue to grow and discover new aspects of yourself.

Finally, remember that embracing change requires patience and self-compassion. Change can be challenging and uncomfortable, but it is also an opportunity for growth and self-discovery. Be kind to yourself as you navigate the ups and downs of change, and trust that each experience is a valuable part of your journey.

7

Chapter 7: Building Resilience

Resilience is the ability to bounce back from challenges and setbacks. It is an essential quality for navigating the inner maze of self-discovery. This chapter will guide you through the process of building resilience and developing the inner strength to overcome obstacles on your journey.

Begin by recognizing the importance of resilience in your life. Resilience allows you to face challenges with confidence and perseverance, turning setbacks into turning points for growth. Embracing resilience allows you to harness your inner strength and keep moving forward, no matter the obstacles you face.

To build resilience, start by cultivating a positive mindset. This doesn't mean ignoring challenges or pretending everything is perfect; rather, it's about focusing on the aspects of your life that bring you joy and fulfillment. Practice gratitude by regularly reflecting on the things you are thankful for, no matter how small. This shift in perspective can help you stay grounded and optimistic, even during tough times.

Another key aspect of building resilience is developing healthy coping strategies. These are the tools and techniques you use to manage stress and navigate difficult situations. Examples include exercise, creative outlets, talking to a trusted friend, or engaging in hobbies. Experiment with different strategies to find what works best for you, and make a conscious effort to incorporate them into your daily routine.

Additionally, building a strong support network is crucial for resilience. Surround yourself with people who uplift and encourage you. This may include friends, family, or support groups. Having a network of supportive individuals can provide you with the emotional strength and guidance you need to overcome challenges.

Lastly, remember that resilience is an ongoing process. It's about learning from setbacks and using those experiences to grow stronger. Approach each challenge with a mindset of growth and self-improvement, and trust in your ability to overcome whatever comes your way.

8

Chapter 8: Cultivating Self-Compassion

Self-compassion is the practice of treating yourself with kindness and understanding, especially during difficult times. It is an essential component of self-discovery, as it allows you to approach your inner journey with a sense of acceptance and love. This chapter will guide you through the process of cultivating self-compassion.

Begin by acknowledging your imperfections and embracing them as a natural part of being human. Everyone makes mistakes, and it is important to approach yourself with the same compassion you would offer a friend. When you experience setbacks or failures, remind yourself that you are not alone and that everyone faces challenges.

Next, practice self-compassion by speaking to yourself with kindness and understanding. Replace self-critical thoughts with supportive and encouraging ones. For example, if you find yourself thinking, "I'm not good enough," reframe it as, "I am doing my best, and that is enough." By changing the way you speak to yourself, you can create a more supportive inner dialogue.

In addition to kind self-talk, engage in self-care practices that nourish your mind, body, and soul. This may include activities such as exercise, meditation, or spending time in nature. Prioritize self-care and make it a regular part of your routine. By taking care of yourself, you can cultivate a greater sense of self-compassion and well-being.

Finally, remember that self-compassion is an ongoing practice. It requires patience and dedication, but the rewards are well worth the effort. By continually practicing self-compassion, you can develop a deeper sense of self-acceptance and love, which will support you on your journey of self-discovery.

9

Chapter 9: Setting Intentions and Goals

Setting intentions and goals is a powerful way to guide your journey of self-discovery. Intentions provide a sense of direction and purpose, while goals give you specific milestones to work towards. This chapter will guide you through the process of setting intentions and goals that align with your true self.

Begin by reflecting on your values and aspirations. What is most important to you? What do you hope to achieve in your life? Take the time to explore these questions and write down your thoughts. This reflection will help you to identify your core intentions and the goals that will support them.

Next, set specific and achievable goals that align with your intentions. These goals should be realistic and attainable, allowing you to make steady progress on your journey. Break down larger goals into smaller, manageable steps, and create a timeline for achieving them. This will help you to stay focused and motivated as you work towards your intentions.

In addition to setting goals, it is important to regularly review and adjust them as needed. Life is constantly changing, and your goals may need to be adapted to reflect new circumstances or insights. By regularly checking in with yourself and adjusting your goals, you can ensure that they remain aligned with your true self.

Finally, remember that setting intentions and goals is not about perfection or achieving specific outcomes. It is about creating a sense of direction and purpose that supports your growth and self-discovery. Embrace the process and be patient with yourself as you work towards your goals.

10

Chapter 10: Embracing Gratitude

Gratitude is a powerful practice that can transform your perspective and enhance your journey of self-discovery. By focusing on the positive aspects of your life, you can cultivate a greater sense of contentment and well-being. This chapter will guide you through the process of embracing gratitude.

Begin by developing a daily gratitude practice. This can be as simple as taking a few moments each day to reflect on the things you are thankful for. You may choose to write them down in a journal or simply take a few moments to think about them. By regularly practicing gratitude, you can shift your focus from what is lacking in your life to what is abundant.

Next, explore the deeper aspects of gratitude by reflecting on the people and experiences that have shaped your life. Consider the ways in which others have supported and influenced you, and take the time to express your gratitude to them. This may involve writing a letter, making a phone call, or simply expressing your appreciation in person.

In addition to personal reflection, engage in acts of kindness and generosity. By giving to others, you can cultivate a greater sense of connection and purpose. Acts of kindness can be small, such as offering a compliment or helping a neighbor, or larger, such as volunteering your time or donating to a cause. Whatever form they take, acts of kindness can help you to cultivate a greater sense of gratitude and fulfillment.

Finally, remember that gratitude is an ongoing practice. It requires regular reflection and effort, but the rewards are well worth it. By continually practicing gratitude, you can develop a greater sense of contentment and well-being, supporting your journey of self-discovery.

11

Chapter 11: Finding Your Purpose

Finding your purpose is a fundamental aspect of self-discovery. It provides a sense of direction and meaning, guiding your actions and decisions. This chapter will guide you through the process of finding your purpose and aligning your life with it.

Begin by reflecting on your passions, values, and strengths. What activities bring you joy and fulfillment? What values are most important to you? What are your unique talents and abilities? By exploring these questions, you can begin to identify the aspects of your life that are most aligned with your true self.

Next, consider the ways in which you can use your passions, values, and strengths to make a positive impact on the world. This may involve pursuing a specific career, engaging in volunteer work, or simply living your life in a way that reflects your values. By aligning your actions with your purpose, you can create a sense of meaning and fulfillment.

In addition to personal reflection, seek out opportunities for growth and exploration. This may involve trying new activities, taking on new challenges, or seeking out new experiences. By continually exploring and expanding your horizons, you can gain new insights into your purpose and how to align your life with it.

Finally, remember that finding your purpose is an ongoing journey. It is not a destination to be reached, but rather a continuous process of growth and self-discovery. Embrace the journey and be patient with yourself as you navigate the path to finding your purpose.

12

Chapter 12: Embracing the Journey

The journey of self-discovery is a lifelong process that requires patience, dedication, and self-compassion. This final chapter will guide you through the process of embracing the journey and continuing to grow and evolve on your path.

Begin by acknowledging the progress you have made and celebrating your achievements. Reflect on the insights you have gained and the ways in which you have grown. By recognizing your progress, you can cultivate a sense of gratitude and motivation to continue on your journey.

Next, commit to ongoing self-reflection and growth. This involves regularly setting aside time for self-reflection, seeking out new experiences, and continuing to challenge yourself. By making self-discovery a regular part of your life, you can ensure that you continue to grow and evolve.

In addition to personal reflection, seek out support and guidance from others. This may involve joining a support group, seeking out a mentor, or simply sharing your journey with a trusted friend. By connecting with others who are also on a path of self-discovery, you can gain valuable insights and support.

Finally, remember that the journey of self-discovery is not about achieving a specific outcome or reaching a final destination. It is about embracing the process and continually seeking to understand yourself and grow. Be patient with yourself and trust in the journey, knowing that each step you take brings you closer to a deeper understanding of your true self.

Book Description:

In a world where external demands often pull us in myriad directions, "Unraveling the Inner Maze: A Guide to Self-Discovery" serves as a beacon of introspection and personal growth. This engaging guide delves deep into the labyrinth of our inner selves, encouraging readers to embark on a transformative journey of self-exploration.

Through twelve thoughtfully crafted chapters, the book takes you on a step-by-step adventure, starting with the essential stages of self-reflection and mindfulness. Each chapter is rich with relatable anecdotes and practical exercises, designed to help you uncover hidden aspects of your personality, understand your past influences, and embrace your true self.

You will learn how to identify and overcome limiting beliefs, build resilience, and cultivate self-compassion. The guide also emphasizes the importance of setting intentions, embracing change, and finding your life's purpose. With a focus on gratitude and a commitment to ongoing growth, "Unraveling the Inner Maze" offers readers the tools to navigate the complexities of their inner world and emerge with a clearer sense of self.

Perfect for anyone at a crossroads or simply curious about their personal potential, this guidebook is an invitation to pause, reflect, and embark on a journey towards a more fulfilling and authentic life.

www.ingramcontent.com/pod-product-compliance
Lightning Source LLC
LaVergne TN
LVHW020744090526
838202LV00057BA/6225